SELF CARE

A Bubble Bath for The Soul
By Aurora Dawn

While every precaution has been taken in the preparation of this book, the publisher assumes no responsibility for errors or omissions, or for damages resulting from the use of the information contained herein.

SELF-CARE: A BUBBLE BATH FOR THE SOUL

First edition. February 14, 2023.

Copyright © 2023 Aurora Dawn.

ISBN: 979-8215491430

Written by Aurora Dawn.

To all the beautiful souls out there, may this book be a gentle reminder to prioritize your self-care and nurture your mind, body, and soul.

You deserve all the love and care in the world.

Introduction:
Why Self-Care is Important

Welcome to 'Self-Care: A Bubble Bath for The Soul.' This book is a guide to help you understand the importance of self-care, and how to make it a priority in your daily life.

Self-care is often thought of as indulgent, or something that can be put off until later. However, the truth is that self-care is essential for both our physical and mental well-being. When we take care of ourselves, we are better able to take care of others and handle the demands of daily life.

In this book, you'll find practical tips and techniques for setting personal boundaries, managing stress, and incorporating self-care into your daily routine. You'll learn about the power of positive thinking, the importance of self-compassion, and how to find your self-care tribe.

We'll also explore the benefits of exercise, nature, mindfulness, and meditation on mental health. We'll look at the relationship between self-care and productivity and how to practice self-care in a busy world.

This book is not only for people who want to improve their self-care habits, but also for those who want to give the gift of self-care to loved ones. It's a perfect guide to give to friends and family members as a reminder of the importance of taking care of themselves.

We hope that 'A Bubble Bath for The Soul' will be a valuable resource for you, and that it will inspire you to make self-care a priority in your life. Now, let's start your self-care journey together.

Setting Personal Boundaries

One of the most important aspects of self-care is setting and maintaining personal boundaries. Personal boundaries are the limits we set for ourselves in order to protect our physical, emotional, and mental well-being. They help us to define who we are and what we will and will not tolerate in our lives.

When we don't set clear boundaries, we can become overwhelmed and exhausted, which can lead to feelings of resentment and burnout. Setting boundaries is an act of self-respect and self-love, and it's essential for maintaining a healthy balance in our relationships and daily life.

Here are some tips for setting and maintaining personal boundaries:

Know your limits: Take some time to reflect on what you are and aren't comfortable with. This includes physical, emotional, and mental boundaries.

Communicate your boundaries clearly: Once you know your limits, make sure to communicate them clearly and assertively to the people in your life. Be prepared to enforce your boundaries if necessary.

Learn to say "no": Saying "no" can be difficult, especially when we want to please others. However, it's essential for maintaining healthy boundaries. Remember that you have the right to say "no" to anything that makes you feel uncomfortable or stressed.

Practice self-care: Taking care of yourself is an important aspect of maintaining boundaries. This includes setting aside time for yourself, engaging in activities that you enjoy, and making sure that you're getting enough rest and nutrition.

Seek help: If you find it difficult to set and maintain boundaries, consider seeking the help of a therapist or counselor.

Setting personal boundaries can be difficult, but it is an important aspect of self-care. Remember that it's not selfish to take care of yourself, it's necessary. By setting clear boundaries, you'll be able to protect yourself and your well-being, and you'll be able to give more to others in the long run.

Another key aspect of setting personal boundaries is learning to recognize when they are being crossed. This can be difficult, especially in situations where the person crossing the boundary is a loved one, or in situations where it's hard to speak up for oneself. However, it's important to remember that you deserve to be treated with respect, and that it's okay to speak up when your boundaries are being crossed.

One way to recognize when your boundaries are being crossed is to pay attention to your feelings. If you feel uncomfortable, resentful, or stressed, it's likely that your boundaries are being crossed. It's important to address these feelings and take action to protect yourself.

Another way to recognize when your boundaries are being crossed is to pay attention to your body. If you notice physical symptoms such as tension, headaches, or stomachaches, it's likely that your boundaries are being crossed.

It's also important to remember that it's okay to change your boundaries as you grow and evolve. What may have been okay in the past may no longer be okay, and it's important to listen to your feelings and adjust your boundaries as needed.

Setting personal boundaries is an essential aspect of self-care. It allows us to define who we are and what we will and will not tolerate in our lives. It helps us to protect our physical, emotional, and mental well-being. Remember to take care of yourself, communicate your boundaries clearly, and seek help when needed.

The Power of Positive Thinking

Positive thinking has been shown to have a powerful impact on our mental and physical health. It can improve our mood, reduce stress, and increase our overall well-being. Positive thinking is the practice of focusing on the good in a situation, rather than dwelling on the negative.

Positive thinking is not about ignoring the negative aspects of life or being unrealistic, but it's about training the mind to focus on the present moment, to see the opportunities and possibilities, and to look for the good in every situation.

Here are some ways to incorporate positive thinking into your daily routine:

- **Practice gratitude**: Take time to reflect on the things in your life that you are grateful for. This can be as simple as writing a list of things you are thankful for each day.
- **Find the positive in every situation**: It's easy to get caught up in the negative aspects of a situation, but try to find the positive. For example, if you're stuck in traffic, you might be frustrated, but instead of dwelling on the delay, you might choose to see it as an opportunity to listen to music or an audio book.
- **Surround yourself with positive people**: The people you spend time with can have a big impact on your mood and outlook. Surround yourself with people who have a positive attitude and who support your goals.
- **Speak positively to yourself**: Our inner dialogue can be

incredibly powerful. Practice speaking positively to yourself, and avoid negative self-talk.

- **Engage in activities that bring you joy**: Do things that make you happy, whether it's reading, painting, or going for a walk. When we engage in activities that bring us joy, it's easier to maintain a positive outlook.

Positive thinking is a skill that can be developed with practice. It's not about ignoring the negative aspects of life, but rather about training the mind to focus on the present moment, to see the opportunities and possibilities, and to look for the good in every situation. By incorporating positive thinking into your daily routine, you can improve your mood, reduce stress, and increase your overall well-being.

Once upon a time, in the kingdom of Arandor, there lived a king named Aric. He was known for his wisdom and kindness, but he had a major flaw, he was a chronic worrier. He worried about everything, from the smallest details of his kingdom to the most insignificant things. His constant worrying began to affect his health and his ability to rule Arandor.

One day, a wise old sage named Zeno came to visit King Aric. Zeno observed the king's constant worrying and knew that he needed to teach him the power of positive thinking.

Zeno told King Aric a story about a farmer named Adair who lived in a small village called Everdale. Adair had a beautiful field of wheat, but he was always worried about the weather, pests and other things that could harm his crops. He would spend hours every day worrying about his field, and as a result, he never truly enjoyed the beauty of his crops.

Zeno then told King Aric about another farmer named Liam who also lived in Everdale. Liam approached his field with a positive attitude. He believed that his crops would be bountiful, and he spent his days working hard and enjoying the beauty of his field. As a result, his crops were always bountiful and healthy.

King Aric was struck by the story, and he realized that he too had been approaching his kingdom with a negative attitude. He decided to change his ways and to adopt a positive attitude. He stopped worrying and started to focus on the good in Arandor. He spent his days working hard and enjoying the beauty of his kingdom. And as a result, his kingdom flourished and his people were happy.

King Aric lived happily ever after and the power of positive thinking became a legend in Arandor.

The moral of the story is that our thoughts and attitudes have a powerful impact on our lives. When we adopt a positive attitude, we are able to see the good in every situation and to find opportunities and possibilities. We can improve our mood, reduce stress and increase our overall well-being. Positive thinking is a skill that can be developed with practice, and it's a powerful tool that can help us to live a happy and fulfilling life.

Finding Your Self-Care Tribe

One of the most important aspects of self-care is having a supportive group of people in your life. These people, also known as your self-care tribe, are the ones who understand and support your self-care journey. They are the ones who will lift you up when you're feeling down, and who will celebrate with you when you achieve your self-care goals.

Having a self-care tribe can make a big difference in your life. Here are some tips for finding and cultivating your self-care tribe:

- **Identify your needs:** Before you can find your self-care tribe, it's important to know what you're looking for. Think about what you need in a supportive group of people. Do you need someone to talk to about your self-care journey, or do you need someone to motivate you to exercise? Knowing what you need will make it easier to find the right people.

- **Look for people with similar interests:** One of the best ways to find your self-care tribe is to look for people who share your interests. This could be a yoga class, a book club, or a running group. Joining a group that shares your interests can be a great way to find like-minded people who will support your self-care journey.

- **Be open to new friendships**: Sometimes, the people who will become our self-care tribe may be unexpected. Be open to new friendships and don't be afraid to reach out to people who may not seem like an obvious fit.

- **Cultivate existing friendships**: Sometimes, the people who will become our self-care tribe are already in our lives. Cultivate existing friendships by talking about your self-care journey and asking for support.

- **Seek professional help**: If you're having trouble finding your self-care tribe, consider seeking the help of a therapist or counselor. They can help you to identify your needs and provide you with strategies for finding a supportive group of people.

Having a self-care tribe can make a big difference in your life. They will support you on your self-care journey, and they will be there to celebrate your achievements. Remember that it's never too late to find your self-care tribe and keep an open mind and heart when seeking them out.

They will be there to celebrate your achievements. An example of this is my friend Samantha, who had always struggled with self-care. She had a hard time setting boundaries and saying no to people. She would often put her own needs last, and as a result, she was always exhausted and stressed.

One day, she decided to make a change and started setting clear boundaries for herself. She joined a local support group for people who were working on self-care, and she started to make new friends. She found people who understood her struggles and who supported her on her self-care journey.

Over time, Samantha found herself becoming more and more confident in setting boundaries and taking care of herself. She started to feel happier and more fulfilled. With the help of her self-care tribe, she was able to achieve her self-care goals and live a happier and healthier life.

Samantha's story is a reminder that we don't have to go through our self-care journey alone. Having a self-care tribe can make a big difference in our lives. They will support us, lift us up when we're feeling down and celebrate with us when we achieve our self-care goals. Remember that finding your self-care tribe is an important aspect of self-care, and it's never too late to start.

The Importance of Self-Compassion

Self-compassion is the practice of being kind and understanding towards oneself during difficult times. It's about treating ourselves with the same kindness, care and understanding that we would offer to a good friend. Self-compassion can be difficult to practice, especially when we are feeling down on ourselves, but it is an essential aspect of self-care.

Here are some ways to practice self-compassion:

- **Be kind to yourself**: Speak to yourself with kindness and understanding. Instead of criticizing yourself, try to offer words of encouragement and support. Take a moment to reflect on the things you're proud of and the things you've accomplished. Write them down and keep them somewhere visible as a reminder of your strengths and capabilities.
- **Practice mindfulness**: Mindfulness is the practice of being present in the moment and observing your thoughts and feelings without judgment. It can help you to be more self-compassionate by allowing you to see your struggles more objectively. Try to take 5 minutes each day for mindfulness practice, such as deep breathing exercises or a short meditation.
- **Recognize that you are not alone**: Remember that everyone goes through difficult times, and that it's normal to struggle. Knowing that you are not alone can help you to be more self-compassionate. Share your struggles with a friend or family member, or join a support group where you can connect with people who understand.

- **Take care of yourself**: Practice self-care activities, such as exercise, meditation, or getting enough sleep, can help to reduce stress and improve your overall well-being. Make a self-care plan, where you can schedule activities that nourish your body and mind, and stick to it.
- **Seek help when needed**: If you're struggling with self-compassion, consider seeking the help of a therapist or counselor. They can provide you with strategies for being more self-compassionate and help you to develop a more positive self-image. Remember that seeking help is not a sign of weakness, but a sign of strength.

Self-compassion is an essential aspect of self-care. It allows us to be kind and understanding towards ourselves during difficult times, and it can help to reduce stress and improve our overall well-being. Remember to be kind to yourself, practice mindfulness, recognize that you are not alone, take care of yourself, and seek help when needed. Take action today, and make self-compassion a daily practice.

Stress Management Techniques

Stress is an inevitable part of life, and it can have a negative impact on our mental and physical health. The key to managing stress is to identify the sources of stress in our lives and to develop effective coping mechanisms. Here are some stress management techniques that can help:

- **Exercise**: Regular exercise is one of the best ways to reduce stress. It releases endorphins, which are chemicals in the brain that improve mood and reduce pain. Aim for at least 30 minutes of exercise per day. For example, going for a daily morning walk or jog, joining a yoga class or even just dancing to your favorite songs for a few minutes can be a great way to start your day.

- **Relaxation techniques**: Relaxation techniques, such as deep breathing, meditation, and yoga, can help to reduce stress and improve overall well-being. Try to take a few minutes each day to practice relaxation techniques. For example, you can try listening to a guided meditation podcast while you commute to work or taking a warm bath with essential oils before bed.

- **Time management:** Stress can often be caused by feeling overwhelmed by a busy schedule. Prioritize your tasks and schedule your time more efficiently. For example, you can try making a to-do list every morning, and focus on the most important tasks first, this way you'll be able to accomplish more in less time and avoid procrastination.

- **Social support**: Having a strong network of friends and family can help to reduce stress. Reach out to your loved ones when you're feeling stressed and don't be afraid to ask for help. For example, you can plan a weekly phone call with a friend, or a monthly dinner with family members, to catch up and talk about your daily life.

- **Mindfulness**: Mindfulness is the practice of being present in the moment and being aware of your thoughts and feelings. It can help to reduce stress by allowing you to see things more objectively. For example, you can try taking a few minutes each day to focus on your breath and observe your thoughts, or simply pay attention to your surroundings while doing your daily activities.

- **Seek professional help**: If stress is interfering with your daily life, consider seeking the help of a therapist or counselor. They can provide you with strategies for managing stress and help you to develop a more positive outlook on life. For example, you can make an appointment with a therapist to talk about your stressors and work on aplan to address them.

It's important to remember that stress management is not a one-time solution, it's a continuous process. Incorporate these techniques into your daily routine and find what works best for you. Experiment with different methods and don't be afraid to try something new. Remember that what works for one person might not work for another, so be patient and keep an open mind. With time and practice, you will be able to manage stress more effectively and live a happier and healthier life. Don't be afraid to reach out for help when you need it, and remember that self-care is vital in the process of stress management.

Creating a Relaxing At-Home Spa Experience

Who doesn't love a relaxing spa day? Unfortunately, not everyone has the time or money to go to a spa regularly. But the good news is, you can create your own spa experience at home. Here are some tips for creating a relaxing spa experience in the comfort of your own home:

- **Set the mood**: Lighting candles, playing soft music and diffusing essential oils can help to create a relaxing and soothing atmosphere. Try to choose scents like lavender, vanilla, or sandalwood to help you relax and unwind.
- **Prepare a warm bath**: Fill your bathtub with warm water and add Epsom salt, baking soda, and a few drops of your favorite essential oils. Soaking in a warm bath can help to relax your muscles and release tension. Try adding rose petals, or a bath bomb to make it even more luxurious.
- **Give yourself a facial**: Treat yourself to a DIY facial by mixing a tablespoon of honey with a teaspoon of turmeric and apply it to your face. Leave it on for 15 minutes before rinsing it off. This will leave your skin feeling smooth and refreshed.
- **Exfoliate your skin**: Dry brush your skin before taking a shower or bath to remove dead skin cells and improve circulation. You can also try using a gentle body scrub or a loofah to exfoliate.
- **Practice self-massage**: Use a massage oil or lotion to give yourself a relaxing massage. Focus on the areas of your body

that feel the most tense. Try using a heated massage oil for an even more relaxing experience.

- **Take a nap:** After your spa experience, take a nap to continue the relaxation and rejuvenation.
- **Enjoy a cup of tea or a healthy snack**: Finish your spa experience by enjoying a cup of tea or a healthy snack. Try making a homemade tea blend with ingredients like chamomile, lemon balm, and lavender, or prepare a small plate of fruits and nuts to enjoy while you relax.
- **Create a designated spa area**: Set aside a specific area in your home where you can go to relax and unwind. It can be a small corner in your bedroom or a dedicated room in your house. Make sure to decorate it with comfortable furniture, soft lighting, and soothing colors.

Creating a relaxing spa experience at home is a great way to take care of yourself and de-stress. Remember to make it a special time for yourself, and don't be afraid to get creative. You can also invite friends and family over to share in the spa experience. The most important thing is to take the time to relax and unwind. So, go ahead and create your own spa day, you deserve it!

The Role of Exercise in Self-Care

Exercise is an essential aspect of self-care. Regular physical activity can help to improve our physical and mental well-being, and it's an effective way to reduce stress and improve mood. Here are some ways that exercise can benefit our self-care:

- **Improves physical health**: Regular exercise can help to improve cardiovascular health, lower blood pressure, and reduce the risk of chronic diseases such as diabetes and heart disease.
- **Boosts mood**: Exercise can help to release endorphins, which are chemicals in the brain that improve mood and reduce pain. This is why many people feel happier and more energized after a workout.
- **Reduces stress**: Exercise can help to reduce stress by releasing tension in the muscles and decreasing the level of stress hormones in the body.
- **Improves sleep:** Regular exercise can help to improve sleep quality and duration.
- **Increases self-esteem**: Regular exercise can help to improve body image and increase self-esteem.
- **Promotes a sense of accomplishment**: Setting and achieving fitness goals can provide a sense of accomplishment and boost confidence.

It's important to find an exercise that you enjoy and that fits your lifestyle. It doesn't have to be a high-intensity workout, it could be something as simple as a daily walk or a yoga class. The key is to make it a regular part of your routine. Remember that the benefits of exercise go beyond just physical health, it can also have a positive impact on our mental and emotional well-being.

Additionally, exercising with a friend or a group can also have a positive impact on our self-care. It can help to boost accountability and motivation, and it can also be a great way to socialize and make new friends.

It's also important to listen to your body and not push yourself too hard. It's okay to take a break if you need it, and to adjust your exercise routine as needed. Remember that self-care is about finding balance, and that includes balancing exercise with rest.

So, make exercise a part of your self-care routine, and you'll be on your way to a happier and healthier you. Remember that self-care is a journey and it takes time and patience, don't be too hard on yourself and enjoy the process.

The Benefits of Nature on Mental Health

Nature has a powerful impact on our mental health. Spending time in nature has been shown to reduce stress, improve mood, and boost overall well-being. Here are some of the benefits of nature on mental health:

- **Reduces stress**: Being in nature can help to reduce stress by decreasing the level of stress hormones in the body.
- **Improves mood:** Spending time in nature can improve mood and promote feelings of happiness and calm.
- **Boosts cognitive function:** Nature has been shown to improve cognitive function, such as attention and memory.
- **Promotes healing and recovery**: Nature has been used as a form of therapy for individuals recovering from illness or injury.
- **Increases self-esteem**: Spending time in nature can improve body image and increase self-esteem.

One of the most powerful ways to experience the benefits of nature on mental health is through a practice called forest bathing, also known as shinrin-yoku. Forest bathing is the practice of immersing yourself in nature, using your senses to connect with the environment. This can include activities such as walking in a forest, listening to the sound of birds, or even just sitting under a tree and taking in the sights and smells.

A story to illustrate the benefits of nature on mental health is the story of Sarah, who was going through a difficult period in her life. She was struggling with depression and anxiety, and her therapist suggested that she try forest bathing. At first, she was skeptical, but she decided to give it a try. She started taking walks in a nearby forest, and she noticed a change in her mood almost immediately. She felt calmer, more relaxed, and happier. As she continued to forest bathe, she noticed that her depression and anxiety began to lift. She felt more connected to herself and to the world around her. She realized that nature was a powerful tool for her mental health and well-being.

It's important to remember that nature is available to all of us, wherever we are. It can be as simple as taking a walk in a local park or even just looking at pictures of nature on your phone. The key is to take the time to connect with nature, and to make it a regular part of your self-care routine. Remember that self-care is a journey and it takes timeand patience, but taking the time to connect with nature can have a profound impact on your mental health and well-being.

It's also important to note that even just viewing nature can have similar benefits. Studies have shown that even just looking at pictures or videos of nature can have a positive impact on our mood and reduce stress. This means that even if you live in an urban area or have limited access to nature, you can still experience the benefits of nature on your mental health.

So, go ahead and take a walk in a nearby park, or simply sit in your backyard and take in the sights and sounds of nature. Make nature a part of your self-care routine and experience the many benefits it has to offer. Remember that self-care is a journey, and it takes time and patience, but connecting with nature can have a profound impact on your mental health and well-being.

Mindfulness and Meditation

Mindfulness and meditation are powerful tools for self-care. They can help to reduce stress, improve mood, and increase overall well-being.

Mindfulness and meditation can be practiced in many different ways. Here are a few examples of exercises that you can try:

- **Body scan**: Lie down or sit comfortably, and focus your attention on each part of your body, starting at the top of your head and working your way down to your toes. Notice any sensations or feelings that come up, and simply observe them without judgment.
- **Breath awareness**: Sit comfortably and focus your attention on your breath. Notice the sensation of the breath as it enters and exits your body. If your mind wanders, simply bring it back to your breath.
- **Loving-kindness meditation**: Sit comfortably and focus on sending love and kindness to yourself and others. Repeat phrases such as "may I be happy, may I be healthy, may I be at peace."
- **Guided meditation**: There are many guided meditations available online, on apps, or on YouTube. These are great for those new to meditation, or for those who find it difficult to focus on their own.

It's important to remember that mindfulness and meditation are not about clearing your mind or getting rid of your thoughts. It's about observing your thoughts without judgment, and bringing your focus back to the present moment.

It's also important to remember that mindfulness and meditation are not one-time solutions. They are a continuous process and it takes time and patience to build the habit. Start with small sessions, and gradually increase the duration. Remember to be kind and compassionate to yourself, and don't be too hard on yourself if your mind wanders during the practice.

Incorporate mindfulness and meditation into your daily routine and see how it can help to improve your mental and emotional well-being. Remember that self-care is a journey and it takes time and patience, but incorporating mindfulness and meditation can have a profound impact on your mental health and well-being.

The Importance of Sleep and How to Improve It

Sleep is essential for our overall well-being, yet many of us struggle to get enough of it. According to the Centers for Disease Control and Prevention, 1 in 3 adults in the United States don't get enough sleep. But the good news is, with a few simple changes, we can improve the quality of our sleep.

Here's why sleep is so important and how you can improve it:

- **Improves physical health**: Sleep is essential for physical health. It helps to repair and rejuvenate the body, and it also helps to lower the risk of chronic diseases such as diabetes and heart disease.
- **Boosts mood**: Sleep is essential for mental health. It helps to improve mood and reduce feelings of anxiety and depression.
- **Enhances cognitive function**: Sleep is essential for cognitive function. It helps to improve memory and concentration, and it also helps to prevent cognitive decline as we age.
- **Increases productivity**: Sleep is essential for productivity. It helps to improve focus and concentration, and it also helps to increase motivation.
- **Improves immune function**: Sleep is essential for immune function. It helps to boost the immune system and reduce the risk of illness and infection.

Sleep is crucial for our overall well-being, yet many of us struggle to get enough of it. But the good news is, with a few simple changes, we can improve the quality of our sleep. Here are a few tips to help you improve your sleep:

- **Stick to a schedule**: Try to go to bed and wake up at the same time every day, even on weekends. This will help to regulate your internal clock.
- **Create a sleep-conducive environment**: Make sure your bedroom is dark, quiet, and cool. Use heavy curtains or blinds to block out light, and use earplugs or a white noise machine to block out noise.
- **Avoid screens before bedtime**: The blue light emitted by screens can interfere with the production of melatonin, the hormone that helps to regulate sleep.
- **Avoid caffeine and alcohol**: Avoid consuming caffeine and alcohol close to bedtime, as they can interfere with sleep.
- **Relax before bedtime:** Try to relax before bedtime. This can include activities such as reading a book, listening to music, or practicing mindfulness and meditation.

Sleep is essential for our overall well-being and it's crucial that we start to treat it like one of the most important things in our lives. It's like the small habit of brushing our teeth before bed, it's something small that we can do every day that has a big impact on our overall health. Just like how a small daily habit of brushing teeth can prevent tooth decay, a small daily habit of getting enough sleep can prevent a host of physical and mental health problems.

Think of sleep as an investment in yourself, just like how you invest money in a savings account. Every night, you deposit time into your sleep account and over time, it will accumulate into a healthy balance of rest and rejuvenation.

It's also important to remember that like any habit, improving sleep takes time and patience. Don't expect to change your sleep habits overnight. Start with small changes, like going to bed and waking up at the same time every day, and gradually build on that. Remember to be kind and compassionate to yourself, and don't be too hard on yourself if you slip up.

Incorporating small changes to your daily routine can make a big impact on your sleep, and ultimately your overall well-being. Remember that self-care is a journey and it takes time and patience, but by prioritizing sleep, you are investing in your physical, mental, and emotional well-being.

Creating a Self-Care Routine
That Works for You

Creating a self-care routine is essential for our overall well-being, but it can be difficult to know where to start. The key is to find what works for you and to make self-care a part of your daily routine. Here are some tips to help you create a self-care routine that works for you:

- **Start small:** Instead of trying to change everything at once, start with one small self-care habit and build on that. For example, start with just taking a few minutes to meditate in the morning or make a warm cup of tea before bed. As you get comfortable with these small habits, you can start to add more self-care activities to your routine.

- **Make it easy:** Make self-care as easy as possible by removing any obstacles that might get in the way. For example, if you want to start a yoga practice, lay out your yoga mat in a spot where you'll see it every day and make sure you have comfortable clothes to wear. This will make it easy to start your practice without having to think too much about it.

- **Prioritize:** Prioritize self-care in your schedule, just like you would with any other important task. Set aside a specific time each day for self-care and make it non-negotiable.

- **Experiment:** Experiment with different self-care activities to find what works best for you. Some people might find yoga to be a great form of self-care, while others may prefer a walk in nature or a relaxing bath.

- **Reflect:** Reflect on your self-care routine and see what works and what doesn't. Make adjustments as needed.
- **Keep it flexible:** Remember that your self-care routine should be flexible, and you should adjust it as needed. Your needs will change over time, and so should your self-care routine. Don't be afraid to try new things and make changes.
- **Make it enjoyable:** Self-care should be enjoyable, so make sure to include activities that you enjoy in your routine. If you don't enjoy meditation, for example, try something else such as journaling or reading.
- **Surround yourself with support:** Surround yourself with people who support and encourage your self-care routine. Share your goals and progress with friends and family and ask for their support.
- **Be consistent:** Consistency is key when it comes to self-care. Try to make self-care a part of your daily routine, and stick to it.
- **Remember** that it's not about reaching perfection but about making progress and taking care of yourself on a daily basis.

Creating a self-care routine that works for you requires some trial and error. It's important to experiment, adjust, and make changes as needed. Remember, self-care is a journey and it takes time and patience. But by incorporating self-care into your daily routine, you are investing in your physical, mental, and emotional well-being. Prioritize yourself and your needs and make self-care a non-negotiable part of your daily routine.

The Relationship Between Self-Care and Productivity

Self-care and productivity are often thought of as separate concepts, but in reality, they are closely linked. Prioritizing self-care and making it a part of your daily routine can actually lead to increased productivity. Here are some examples of how self-care can improve your productivity:

- **A good night's sleep:** Taking care of your physical well-being by getting a good night's sleep can improve your focus and concentration, making you more productive during the day.
- **Exercise:** Regular exercise not only improves physical health, but it also improves cognitive function, reduces stress and increases energy levels, all of which can lead to increased productivity.
- **Mindfulness:** Mindfulness practices such as meditation and yoga can help to reduce stress and improve mental clarity, leading to increased productivity.
- **Eat well:** Eating well-balanced meals can improve your energy levels, focus and overall well-being, which can lead to increased productivity.
- **Time management:** Prioritizing self-care by taking regular breaks and time management techniques such as the Pomodoro technique, can help increase productivity by reducing burnout and fatigue.

- **Organizing your work environment**: Having a clean and well-organized work environment can improve focus and productivity.
- **Prioritizing important tasks**: Prioritizing important tasks and focusing on them can help increase productivity and achieve better results.
- **Building a support system**: Building a support system of friends and family who understand and support your self-care and productivity goals can help you stay motivated and on track.

Self-care is not about taking time away from productivity, but rather, it's about making sure that you're taking care of yourself so that you can be more productive in the long run. By incorporating self-care into your daily routine, you can improve your physical, mental, and emotional well-being, which in turn can lead to increased productivity. Remember, self-care is a journey and it takes time and patience, but by making small changes, you can see big improvements in your productivity.

It's important to experiment with different self-care practices and find what works best for you. For example, if you find that exercise helps you to focus better and increases your energy levels, make sure to include it in your daily routine. Similarly, if you find that taking regular breaks throughout the day helps you to stay focused, make sure to schedule them in.

Also, it's important to be flexible and adjust your self-care routine as needed. Your needs will change over time, so make sure to re-evaluate your routine regularly and make changes as needed.

In summary, self-care and productivity are closely linked and by prioritizing self-care and making it a part of your daily routine, you can increase your productivity and overall well-being. Remember to experiment with different self-care practices, be flexible and adjust your routine as needed, and build a support system to help you stay motivated and on track.

The Power of a Morning Routine: Setting the Tone for the Day

There's something magical about the morning, it's a fresh start, a new beginning, an opportunity to set the tone for the rest of the day. And what better way to start the day than with a morning routine?

A morning routine is a series of activities that you do every morning to set yourself up for success. It's a way to start the day on the right foot and to set a positive tone for the rest of the day. It's a way to take control of your day and to make sure that you're starting it on your terms.

The benefits of a morning routine are numerous. A morning routine can help to improve your productivity, boost your mood, and increase your overall well-being. It can also help to reduce stress and anxiety and to improve your sleep.

One of the keys to creating a successful morning routine is to make sure that it's tailored to your unique needs. It's important to find activities that work for you and that align with your goals and values. It's also important to make sure that your morning routine is realistic and that it fits into your lifestyle.

Another key to creating a successful morning routine is to make sure that it's consistent. Consistency is key when it comes to building habits, and a morning routine is no exception. By making sure that you do the same things every morning, you'll find that it becomes easier and easier to do them.

Here are some steps to help you create a successful morning routine:

- Start by identifying your goals and values.
- Experiment with different activities and find what works for you.
- Make sure that your morning routine is realistic and that it fits into your lifestyle.
- Be consistent with your morning routine and make it a habit.

In conclusion, a morning routine is a powerful tool for setting the tone for the day. It can help to improve your productivity, boost your mood, and increase your overall well-being. The key to creating a successful morning routine is to make sure that it's tailored to your unique needs, that it's realistic and that it's consistent. Remember, the power of a morning routine lies in its ability to set the tone for the day, and it's a powerful tool for creating a positive change in your life. Wake up early, plan your morning routine and start your day off right!

How to Practice Self-Care
in a Busy World

In today's fast-paced world, it can be difficult to find time for self-care. We are always on the go, and it can feel like there are not enough hours in the day to take care of ourselves. But the truth is, self-care is just as important in a busy world as it is in a less hectic one. The key is to find ways to make self-care a priority, even amidst the busyness of life.

One way to do this is by setting aside specific time each day for self-care. This could be something as simple as a five-minute meditation in the morning or a relaxing bath before bed. While these may seem like small acts, they can make a big difference in how we feel throughout the day. Another way to make self-care a priority is by being mindful of how we spend our time. It can be easy to get caught up in the busyness of life and forget to take care of ourselves. By being mindful of our time and making sure that self-care is a priority, we can ensure that we are taking care of ourselves amidst the busyness.

It's important to remember that self-care doesn't have to be a big, time-consuming task. It can be as simple as taking a few deep breaths, or drinking a glass of water. It's about finding small ways to take care of ourselves amidst the busyness of life.

A great way to make self-care a priority in a busy world is by creating a self-care routine. A self-care routine is a set of activities that you do regularly to take care of yourself. This routine can include things like exercise, meditation, journaling, reading, or whatever else makes you feel good. By creating a self-care routine and sticking to it, you are making self-care a non-negotiable part of your daily routine, which helps to ensure that you are taking care of yourself amidst the busyness of life.

Let's take the example of Jane, a working mother who is always on the go. Between her job, her kids, and the household chores, Jane never has a moment to herself. She's always tired, and she starts to realize that she's not taking care of herself. She starts experimenting with small self-care activities, like taking a few deep breaths or drinking a glass of water, and she starts to notice a big change in how she feels. She starts to feel better, less stressed, and more energized.

Encouraged by her small successes, Jane starts to incorporate more self-care activities into her daily routine. She makes a habit of meditating for 5 minutes before bed, and starts going for a walk during her lunch break. She also starts to prioritize time for herself on the weekends, by scheduling a yoga class or a spa day. By creating a self-care routine and sticking to it, she's making self-care a non-negotiable part of her daily routine, which helps to ensure that she is taking care of herself amidst the busyness of life.

Jane's experience shows that self-care is not about taking time away from your busy life, but rather, it's about making sure that you're taking care of yourself so that you can be more productive and present in your busy life. By incorporating small self-care practices into your daily routine, you can ensure that you are taking care of yourself amidst the busyness of life.

Remember, self-care is not about taking time away from your busy life, but rather, it's about making sure that you're taking care of yourself so that you can be more productive and present in your busy life. By incorporating small self-care practices into your daily routine, you can ensure that you are taking care of yourself amidst the busyness of life.

It's important to remember that self—care doesn't have to be a big, time-consuming task. It can be as simple as taking a few deep breaths, or drinking a glass of water. It's about finding small ways to take care of ourselves amidst the busyness of life. And it's important to be mindful of your time and make self-care a priority, even amidst the busyness of life.

Creating a self-care routine and sticking to it, can make all the difference. Whether it's taking a few minutes to meditate, going for a walk during lunch break, or scheduling a yoga class on the weekends, incorporating self-care into your daily routine can help you to prioritize your well-being, and make you more productive and present in your busy life.

As Jane discovered, self-care is a journey, it takes time and patience but by making small changes, you can see big improvements in your overall well-being. So, take inspiration from Jane's story, and start incorporating small self-care practices into your daily routine, and see the difference it makes in your busy life.

The Importance of Self-Reflection

Self-reflection is the process of taking a step back and evaluating our thoughts, feelings, and actions. It's about taking the time to understand ourselves better and gain insight into our behavior, emotions and thought patterns. Many of us go through life without taking the time to reflect on who we are and what we want. But self-reflection is an essential part of self-care, and it's important to make it a regular practice in order to understand and improve ourselves.

It's easy to get caught up in the day-to-day demands of life, and before we know it, weeks, months, or even years have gone by without taking the time to reflect on who we are and what we want. But when we take the time to reflect on our lives, we gain a better understanding of ourselves, our thoughts, emotions and actions. We can see patterns that we may not have noticed before, and we can start to make changes that will improve our overall well-being.

Self-reflection is also important because it allows us to take responsibility for our actions. It's easy to blame others or external factors for our problems, but by reflecting on our thoughts, feelings and actions, we can take ownership of our lives and make changes that will lead to a more fulfilling life.

A great way to start self-reflection is by journaling. Writing down your thoughts and feelings can help you gain insight into yourself and your behavior. You can also try meditation or therapy, which can help you gain a deeper understanding of yourself.

It's important to remember that self-reflection is not about being hard on yourself, but rather, it's about being honest with yourself and making changes that will lead to a more fulfilling life. So, make self-reflection a regular practice, whether it's through journaling, meditation, or therapy, and start to gain a deeper understanding of yourself, your thoughts, feelings, and actions.

Here are some questions you can ask yourself to help you self-reflect:

- *What are my core values?*
- *How have I been feeling lately? Why?*
- *What are my strengths and weaknesses?*
- *How have my actions aligned with my values and goals?*
- *What would I like to change about myself?*
- *What are the things I am grateful for?*
- *What are the things I want to do differently?*

Self-reflection is an essential tool for self-care, personal growth and development. It enables us to understand our thoughts, emotions, behavior, and actions. It allows us to take ownership of our lives and make changes that will lead to a more fulfilling and satisfying life. Start today by taking a few minutes to reflect on your thoughts, feelings, and actions, and see the difference it makes in your overall well-being.

The Art of Self-Forgiveness

We all make mistakes. We all have moments of weakness and moments when we fall short of our own expectations. It's part of being human. But, what happens when those mistakes or weaknesses continue to haunt us? How do we move on and forgive ourselves for our past actions?

Self-forgiveness is not about excusing or forgetting our actions. It's about acknowledging what we've done, taking responsibility, and making amends where possible. It's about letting go of the past and learning to be kind and compassionate to ourselves.

For many of us, self-forgiveness is hard because we hold ourselves to an impossible standard of perfection. We beat ourselves up over small mistakes and constantly replay past events in our minds. We compare ourselves to others and focus on our weaknesses, rather than our strengths. But, this kind of thinking only leads to feelings of inadequacy and self-doubt.

Instead of focusing on perfection, we should focus on progress. We can't change the past, but we can learn from it and use it as a tool for growth. We can take the lessons we've learned and apply them to our lives moving forward. We can strive to be better, but not perfect.

It's important to remember that self-forgiveness is not a one-time event. It's a process that takes time and patience. It's about learning to be kind and compassionate to ourselves, even when we make mistakes. It's about learning to let go of the past and focus on the present.

Here are some steps that can help you on your journey towards self-forgiveness:

- Acknowledge your mistake and take responsibility for it.
- Make amends where possible.
- Learn from the experience and use it as a tool for growth.
- Practice self-compassion. Be kind and understanding towards yourself.
- Let go of the past and focus on the present.

In conclusion, self-forgiveness is about acknowledging our mistakes, taking responsibility for them, and learning to be kind and compassionate towards ourselves. It's about letting go of the past and focusing on the present. Remember, self-forgiveness is not a one-time event, it's a process that takes time and patience. Be gentle with yourself, be kind, and remember that you are worthy of forgiveness.

Embracing Imperfection:
The Key to Self-Acceptance

In today's society, we are constantly bombarded with images of perfection. Whether it's on social media, in magazines, or on television, we are presented with an idealized version of what we should look like, act like, and achieve. It's easy to fall into the trap of comparing ourselves to these ideals and feeling like we fall short. But what if we were to embrace our imperfections instead of trying to hide or change them?

Embracing imperfection is about learning to accept and love ourselves for who we are, flaws and all. It's about recognizing that perfection is an illusion and that everyone has imperfections. It's about understanding that our imperfections are what make us unique and that they are a part of what makes us human.

One of the keys to embracing imperfection is to focus on self-acceptance. Self-acceptance is about learning to accept yourself for who you are, without judgment or criticism. It's about recognizing that everyone is different and that there is no one "right" way to be. It's about understanding that our imperfections are not something to be ashamed of, but something to be celebrated.

Another key to embracing imperfection is learning to let go of the need to control everything. We can't control everything that happens in our lives, and we can't control how others see us. We can only control how we see ourselves. By letting go of the need to control everything, we can learn to be more present in the moment and to appreciate the beauty in the imperfect.

Here are some steps that can help you on your journey towards embracing imperfection:

- Recognize that perfection is an illusion and that everyone has imperfections.
- Practice self-acceptance, learn to accept yourself for who you are, without judgment or criticism.
- Let go of the need to control everything.
- Be present in the moment and appreciate the beauty in the imperfect.

In conclusion, embracing imperfection is about learning to accept and love ourselves for who we are, flaws and all. It's about recognizing that perfection is an illusion and that everyone has imperfections. It's about understanding that our imperfections are what make us unique and that they are a part of what makes us human. By focusing on self-acceptance, letting go of the need to control everything and being present in the moment, we can learn to embrace our imperfections and to find beauty in them. Remember, you are unique and that's something special, embrace it.

Healing through Creativity: Using the Arts for Self-Expression

Creativity is a powerful tool for self-expression and self-discovery. It's a way to tap into our innermost thoughts, emotions, and feelings and to turn them into something tangible and real. And when it comes to self-care, creativity can be an incredibly powerful tool for healing and growth.

The arts offer a wide range of outlets for self-expression, from writing and painting to music and dance. Each medium has its own unique way of allowing us to express ourselves and to connect with our inner selves. For example, writing can be a powerful tool for exploring our thoughts and emotions, while painting can be a way to visually express our feelings. Music and dance, on the other hand, can be a way to release pent-up emotions and to connect with our bodies.

Creativity also allows us to tap into our imagination and to explore new possibilities. It allows us to step out of our comfort zones and to try new things. It also allows us to see the world in new ways and to find new solutions to old problems.

One of the keys to using creativity for self-care is to set aside dedicated time for it. This means making time in your schedule for creative pursuits, whether it's an hour a day, a few hours a week, or whatever works best for you. It's also important to be open to new experiences and to try different types of art and creative expression.

Another key to using creativity for self-care is to let go of perfectionism and to allow yourself to make mistakes. Creativity is about experimenting, making mistakes, and learning from them. By letting go of the need to create something perfect, you open yourself up to new possibilities and new ways of expressing yourself.

Here are some steps to help you use creativity for self-care:

- Set aside dedicated time for creative pursuits
- Try different types of art and creative expression
- Let go of perfectionism and allow yourself to make mistakes
- Use your creativity as a tool for self-expression and self-discovery.

Using the arts as a form of self-expression and self-discovery can be a powerful tool for healing and growth. The key is to set aside dedicated time for creative pursuits, to try different types of art, and to let go of perfectionism. Whether you're a writer, painter, musician or dancer, the key is to use your creativity to express yourself, to tap into your imagination, and to explore new possibilities. Remember, the beauty of the arts is that they allow us to turn the intangible into something tangible, and in the process, we can heal, grow and learn more about ourselves.

The Power of Gratitude

Gratitude is the practice of being thankful for the good things in our lives. It's about taking the time to appreciate the people, experiences, and things that bring us joy and make our lives better. By cultivating a grateful attitude, we can improve our overall well-being and find happiness in the present moment.

Many of us go through life focusing on what we don't have, rather than what we do have. We become so wrapped up in our own wants and needs that we fail to appreciate the good things in our lives. But when we start to practice gratitude, we shift our focus from what we lack to what we have, and we start to see the good in our lives.

One of the best ways to practice gratitude is by keeping a gratitude journal. Every day, take a few minutes to write down three things you're grateful for. They can be big or small, it doesn't matter. The act of writing them down helps to solidify them in your mind, and over time, you'll start to notice a shift in your attitude towards life.

Let me tell you a story of a man named Jack. Jack was going through a difficult time in his life. He had lost his job, and he was struggling to make ends meet. He felt like he had nothing to be grateful for. But one day, a friend suggested he start a gratitude journal. At first, Jack was skeptical. He didn't think there was anything in his life to be grateful for. But he decided to give it a try.

Every day, he would write down three things he was grateful for. Some days, it was as simple as the sun shining or a good cup of coffee. Other days, it was something bigger, like a kind word from a stranger or a small act of kindness from a friend.

As the weeks went by, Jack started to notice a shift in his attitude. He began to see the good in his life, even amidst the difficulties. He started to feel more hopeful and less stressed. His gratitude journal had become a source of comfort and inspiration, and it helped him to appreciate the small things in life.

Gratitude is a powerful tool for self-care, it can help us to appreciate the good things in our lives and shift our focus from what we lack to what we have. It can help us to find happiness in the present moment, and it can improve our overall well-being. Start today by keeping a gratitude journal, and see the difference it makes in your life.

Overcoming Negative Self-Talk

Negative self-talk is a common problem that many of us experience. It's when we have negative thoughts and beliefs about ourselves that can hold us back in life. Negative self-talk can manifest in many ways, such as feeling inadequate, unworthy, or not good enough. It can also lead to feelings of depression, anxiety and low self-esteem. But the good news is that it can be overcome.

The first step in overcoming negative self-talk is to become aware of it. Negative self-talk often happens unconsciously, and we may not even realize we're doing it. But once we become aware of it, we can start to take steps to change it.

One way to do this is by reframing our thoughts. When we catch ourselves having negative thoughts, we can try to reframe them in a more positive light. For example, instead of thinking "I'm not good enough," we can try to reframe it as "I am capable and have the ability to improve."

Another way to overcome negative self-talk is through the practice of mindfulness. Mindfulness is the practice of being present in the moment and not getting caught up in our thoughts. When we're mindful, we're less likely to get caught up in negative self-talk because we're more focused on the present moment.

It's also important to surround yourself with positive people who will support and encourage you. Negative self-talk can be reinforced by the people we surround ourselves with, so it's important to be around those who will uplift and support us.

In addition, self-compassion is a powerful tool in overcoming negative self-talk. Self-compassion involves treating ourselves with kindness and understanding rather than judgment and criticism. When we're compassionate towards ourselves, we're less likely to engage in negative self-talk.

Lastly, therapy and counseling can also be a helpful tool in overcoming negative self-talk. A therapist can help you identify and understand the underlying causes of your negative self-talk and provide you with strategies to overcome it.

In conclusion, negative self-talk can be an obstacle in our lives, but it can be overcome. By becoming aware of it, reframing our thoughts, practicing mindfulness, surrounding ourselves with positive people, being self-compassionate and seeking therapy or counseling, we can learn to quiet the negative voice in our heads and focus on the positive. Remember, negative self-talk is not a reflection of reality, but rather a habit of the mind that can be changed. It may take time and consistent effort, but with patience and persistence, you can learn to overcome negative self-talk and improve your overall well-being.

The Benefits of Journaling for Self-Care

Journaling is a simple yet powerful tool for self-care. It's a way to express your thoughts, feelings, and experiences in a private and safe space. By putting your thoughts and emotions on paper, you can gain insight and understanding into yourself and your life. Journaling can also provide an outlet for stress, anxiety, and other negative emotions.

One of the benefits of journaling for self-care is that it can help to clarify your thoughts and feelings. When we're going through a difficult time, it can be hard to make sense of what we're feeling. Journaling can provide a way to process and understand our emotions, which can help us to feel more in control of our lives.

Journaling can also be a great way to track your progress and set goals. By writing down your goals, you can make them more concrete, and by keeping track of your progress, you can see how far you've come and celebrate your accomplishments. This can be a great way to build momentum and motivation towards achieving your goals.

Another benefit of journaling for self-care is that it can be a great way to relieve stress and anxiety. Writing about what's on your mind can help you to release pent-up emotions and feelings, which can help you to feel more relaxed and at ease.

Journaling can also be a great way to practice gratitude and focus on the positive things in your life. By writing down things you're grateful for, you can shift your focus from what you lack to what you have, and you'll start to see the good in your life.

Here are some tips to get you started with journaling for self-care:

- Start by setting aside a specific time each day or each week to journal. This can be first thing in the morning, before bed, or during your lunch break.
- Use prompts to help you get started. You can find journal prompts online or create your own.
- Keep it simple. You don't have to write a novel, just write down whatever comes to mind.
- Be honest and authentic. Don't hold back, write down what you're really thinking and feeling.
- Be consistent. The more you journal, the more benefits you'll see.

In conclusion, journaling is a simple yet powerful tool for self-care. It provides a way to express your thoughts, feelings, and experiences in a private and safe space. It can help you to clarify your thoughts and feelings, track your progress and set goals, relieve stress and anxiety, practice gratitude, and focus on the positive things in your life. Give it a try and see how journaling can improve your overall well-being.

The Importance of Play in Self-Care

We often think of self-care as being serious and focused on taking care of our physical and mental health. However, play is an essential aspect of self-care that is often overlooked. Play is not just for children, it's a vital part of self-care for people of all ages.

Play is defined as an activity that is done for enjoyment and leisure. It's about having fun, letting go of stress and worries, and embracing the present moment. Play allows us to tap into our imagination, to be spontaneous, and to let go of our inhibitions. It also allows us to connect with others and to build relationships.

Play has many benefits for our physical and mental health. It can help to reduce stress and anxiety, to boost our mood and to improve our overall well-being. It can also help to improve our cognitive function and to boost our creativity.

One of the keys to incorporating play into your self-care routine is to make time for it. This means setting aside dedicated time for play, whether it's an hour a day, a few hours a week, or whatever works best for you. It's also important to be open to new experiences and to try different types of play.

Another key to incorporating play into your self-care routine is to let go of perfectionism. Play is not about achieving a specific goal or outcome, it's about having fun and enjoying the present moment. By letting go of the need to be perfect, you open yourself up to new possibilities and new ways of having fun.

Here are some steps to help you incorporate play into your self-care routine:

- Set aside dedicated time for play
- Try different types of play
- Let go of perfectionism
- Use play as a tool for reducing stress and boosting your mood

All in all, play is an essential aspect of self-care that is often overlooked. It's not just for children, it's a vital part of self-care for people of all ages. Play allows us to tap into our imagination, to be spontaneous, and to let go of our inhibitions. It also allows us to connect with others and to build relationships. Incorporating play into your self-care routine can help to reduce stress and anxiety, to boost your mood, and to improve your overall well-being. The key is to make time for it, to be open to new experiences, and to let go of perfectionism. Remember to have fun, laugh, play and let loose!

Self-Care for Caregivers

Being a caregiver can be a taxing and onerous responsibility. Whether you're looking after a family member with a chronic condition, an aging parent, or a child with special needs, it can take its toll on your physical, emotional and mental well-being. It's imperative to take care of yourself while you're taking care of others. This is where self-care comes in.

One of the most crucial things you can do for yourself as a caregiver is to establish boundaries. It's vital to make time for yourself and your own needs. This might mean declining certain duties or assigning tasks to others. It's essential to remember that you can't pour from an empty vessel.

Another essential aspect of self-care for caregivers is to maintain your physical health. This might mean making time for regular physical activity, eating healthily, and getting enough sleep. It's also vital to make sure you're taking care of your own medical needs. This will not only keep you healthy, but it will also make you a better caregiver.

It's also vital to make time for yourself and to engage in activities that bring you pleasure. This might mean taking a yoga class, going for a hike in nature, or reading a book. It's vital to make time for yourself and to engage in activities that you enjoy, this will help you to recharge and feel more balanced.

It's also essential to seek out support from others. This might mean joining a support group for caregivers, talking to a therapist, or seeking support from friends and family. It's vital to remember that you're not alone in your journey, and that there are people who care about you and want to help.

Lastly, it's essential to remember to be kind and compassionate towards yourself. As a caregiver, it's easy to be hard on yourself for not doing enough or for not being perfect. Remember that you're doing the best you can, and that it's okay to make mistakes.

In conclusion, self-care is crucial for caregivers. It's vital to establish boundaries, maintain your physical health, make time for yourself, seek out support, and be kind and compassionate towards yourself. Caring for yourself will not only help you to be a better caregiver, but it will also improve your overall well-being. Remember to take care of yourself, so you can be there to take care of others.

Closing Thoughts:
Making Self-Care a Priority

As you come to the end of this book, I hope that you have gained a deeper understanding of the importance of self-care and how to make it a priority in your life. We have covered a wide range of topics, from setting personal boundaries and positive thinking to finding your self-care tribe and the importance of sleep. We have also talked about stress management techniques, creating a relaxing at-home spa experience, the role of exercise in self-care, the benefits of nature on mental health, mindfulness and meditation, journaling, and self-care for caregivers.

Self-care is not a one-size-fits-all concept, and what works for one person may not work for another. The key is to find what works for you and to make it a priority in your life. This means setting aside dedicated time for self-care, whether it's an hour a day, a few hours a week, or whatever works best for you. It's also important to be open to new experiences and to try different types of self-care.

Incorporating self-care into your daily routine can be challenging, but it's important to remember that self-care is not selfish, it's essential for your overall well-being. Self-care allows you to recharge and to take care of yourself, so that you can be the best version of yourself for the people around you.

As you close this book, I encourage you to reflect on the topics covered and to think about how you can incorporate self-care into your life. Remember that self-care is not a one-time thing, it's an ongoing process. It's about making self-care a priority in your life and taking small steps to make it a part of your daily routine.

I hope that this book has been helpful and that you have found something that resonates with you. Remember, self-care is an ongoing journey, and it's a journey that you don't have to take alone. There are many people who care about you and who want to support you.

In closing, I want to thank you for reading this book and for making the effort to take care of yourself. Remember that you are worthy of self-care and that it's essential for your overall well-being. I hope that this book has helped you understand yourself and your needs better and that you will continue to make self-care a priority in your life.

SELF-CARE: A BUBBLE BATH FOR THE SOUL

As you close this book, remember to take a deep breath, let go of any bubbles of stress and worries and allow yourself to fully immerse in the warm embrace of self-care, because you deserve nothing but the best, a bubble bath for the soul.

63